The Let's Talk Library™

Let's Talk About
Diabetes

Melanie Apel Gordon

The Rosen Publishing Group's
PowerKids Press™
New York

For Richard, my one and only . . . Love, MAGS

Published in 1999 by The Rosen Publishing Group, Inc.
29 East 21st Street, New York, NY 10010

First Edition

Book Design: Erin McKenna

Photo Credits: Cover and photo illustrations pp. 4, 8, 11, 12, 16, 20 by Seth Dinnerman; p. 7 © PhotoDisc; p. 15 © Custom Medical Stock Photo; p. 19 by Guillerminade Ferrari

Gordon, Melanie Apel.
    Let's talk about diabetes / by Melanie Apel Gordon
        p.   cm. — (The Let's talk library)
    Includes index.
    Summary: A simple introduction to the symptoms of diabetes, its effects on the body, and how it is controlled with diet and insulin.
    ISBN 0-8239-5196-0
    1. Diabetes—Juvenile literature. 2. Diabetes in children—Juvenile literature.   I. Title. II. Series.
RC660.5.G67   1998
616.4'62—dc21   97-38705
                                                                                           CIP
                                                                                            AC

Manufactured in the United States of America

Table of Contents

POTD

① There are 15 people at a party. If each person shakes hands once with everyone at the party, how many handshakes will there be?

② 4.28
  × .35

Sasha

The clock on the classroom wall looks blurry, but Sasha can still see that it says 11:30—a half hour until lunchtime. She's hungry and very thirsty. Sasha wiggles in her seat. She really has to use the bathroom. She doesn't want to ask her teacher if she can go again. She just went to the bathroom a few minutes ago. What's wrong with me? Sasha wonders.

◀ If your body is acting funny, tell your parents or your teacher right away.

Diabetes

Diabetes (dy-uh-BEE-teez) is when your body can't use **glucose** (GLOO-kohs) correctly. Glucose is a sugar that your body uses for energy. You get glucose from the foods you eat. When you have diabetes your body does not make enough **insulin** (IN-suh-lin). Insulin is a **hormone** (HOR-mohn) made by your body that helps your body to use glucose. If your body can't use the glucose you eat, it comes out in your **urine** (YER-in). This can make you feel dizzy, thirsty, and sick.

Fruits, such as grapes, apples, and peaches, ▶ have lots of sugar in them.

How Do Kids Get Diabetes?

Doctors do not know exactly why kids get diabetes. They think kids may sometimes get diabetes from a virus. A virus is a germ that makes you sick, like when you get a cold. If the virus gets into your **pancreas** (PAYN-kree-is), it can hurt the cells that make insulin. If this happens then you can get diabetes. But this does not happen often. Just because you have a cold doesn't mean that you will get diabetes. It's important to know that you can't catch diabetes from someone who has it.

◀ You can lead a normal life with diabetes.

Insulin Shots

Some diabetics cannot **digest** (dy-JEST) glucose unless they give themselves insulin shots every day. First, they test the glucose in their blood—called blood sugar—with a special kit. Then they give themselves a shot. They may do this before meals and at bedtime. But every **diabetic** (dy-uh-BEH-tik) is different and has his or her own special time for insulin. It's important for his or her blood sugar to be just right. Insulin shots will keep a diabetic's blood sugar at healthy levels.

Even though a person with diabetes has to have shots a couple of times a day, she gets used to them. ▶

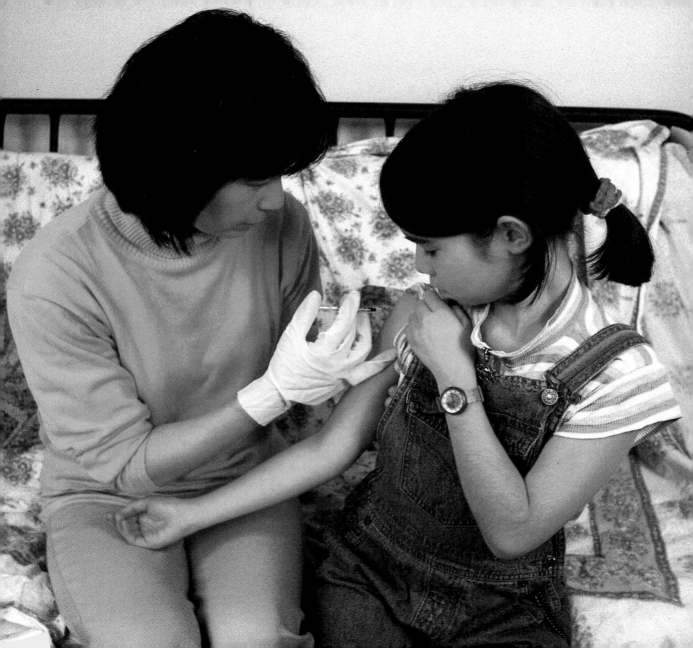

Eating

What kind of foods and when you eat are very important when you have diabetes. You should eat well-balanced meals. And you should eat regularly. Never skip a meal. Your doctor can help you plan healthful meals. And you should stay away from candy and other foods and drinks that have a lot of sugar in them. Vegetables, bread, meat, and fish are good foods to eat. It's also good to eat low fat food. Your whole family will be healthier if they follow this diet with you.

◀ Eating healthy foods is important for everyone, whether a person has diabetes or not.

Too Much Sugar

If you are diabetic and eat too much or do not take enough insulin, you could get **ketoacidosis** (KEE-toh-as-ih-DOH-sis). This happens when there is too much sugar in your blood. You may feel sick, extra thirsty, itchy, very tired, or have trouble breathing. Diabetics test their urine with special strips to make sure they do not have ketoacidosis. If the test says they have ketoacidosis, they should call the doctor right away!

If someone has ketoacidosis there will be glucose in his or her urine. ▶

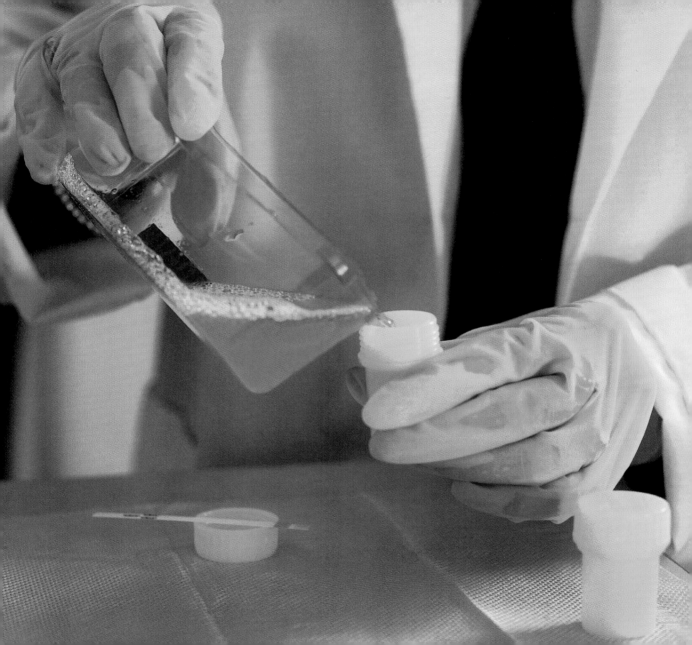

Low Blood Sugar

If you are diabetic and your blood sugar gets too low, it is called **hypoglycemia** (HY-poh-gly-SEE-mee-uh). This happens if you take too much insulin, if you don't eat enough, or if you skip a meal. When your blood sugar is low, you may feel shaky, hungry, tired, or nervous. You can fix hypoglycemia by drinking juice or milk or by eating candy or fruit. This is the one time when it is okay to eat food with sugar in it. After you feel better, you should eat a healthful, nonsugary snack.

◀ When your blood sugar is low, drinking milk is a good, healthy way to make you feel better.

Who Gets Diabetes?

Anyone can get diabetes. But only one out of every 200 kids has it. There are two kinds of diabetes. The kind that kids sometimes get is called Type I. If you have Type I diabetes, you need shots of insulin to help your body use glucose. Type II diabetes is the kind that some grown-ups get. Eating a healthful diet and getting exercise is usually enough to keep Type II diabetics healthy. But sometimes Type II diabetics need to take insulin shots.

Kids with diabetes are just the same as kids without diabetes; they just have to watch what they eat. ▶

Diabetes Is Serious

When you get diabetes, you have it for the rest of your life. There is no cure for it yet. If you have diabetes you need to exercise, watch what you eat, and remember to take your insulin. If you don't take care of yourself, diabetes can be harmful. Over time it can cause problems in your eyes, your legs and feet, your heart, and your **kidneys** (KID-neez). But you will live a long, healthy life with diabetes as long as you take care of yourself.

◀ Eating right and exercising will keep your body healthy.

A Regular Kid

Diabetics know that their diabetes is serious and it won't go away. They test their blood sugar and take insulin shots. They are careful about the foods they eat and remember to eat on time. And they exercise. Kids who have diabetes are regular kids, but they have extra **responsibilities** (ree-spon-sih-BIL-ih-teez). They like to do the same things that their friends like to do. Diabetes won't change that. If diabetics remember to take care of their bodies, then their bodies will take care of them!

Glossary

diabetes (dy-uh-BEE-teez) When the body can't digest glucose.

diabetic (dy-uh-BEH-tik) A person who has diabetes.

digest (dy-JEST) When your body uses the food you eat for energy.

glucose (GLOO-kohs) The sugar your body uses for energy.

hormone (HOR-mohn) A chemical in your body that helps your cells do their job.

hypoglycemia (HY-poh-gly-SEE-mee-uh) When there is not enough sugar in your blood.

insulin (IN-suh-lin) A hormone that helps your cells use glucose.

ketoacidosis (KEE-toh-as-ih-DOH-sis) When there is too much sugar in your blood.

kidneys (KID-neez) Organs in your body that filter waste products from your blood so they can leave your body through your urine.

pancreas (PAYN-kree-is) An organ in your body that makes insulin.

responsibility (ree-spon-sih-BIL-ih-tee) Something that you do to take care of yourself.

urine (YER-in) The waste from your body that comes out as pee.

Index